I0217713

The Little Gate of the Great King

The Real Story of Christmas

by Colin Baker

*****

from The Gates of the Kingdom Book Series

Published in Australia by Kingdomgates Publishing © 2012 Colin Baker. All rights reserved. No copy of this book may be reproduced, stored in a retrieval system, or transmitted in any form or by any means – electronic, mechanical, photocopy, recording, scanning, or other – except for brief quotations, without obtaining prior written permission of the publisher.

ISBN: 1922223956

ISBN-13: 9781922223951

from The Gates of the Kingdom Book Series

Dedicated to the Great King, our glorious Lord and Savior, Yeshua the Messiah; Adonai Kabod; the Lord of Glory.

* * * * *

Colin Russell Baker

Contents

Part 1 5

Part 2 17

Part 3 41

Part 4 61

from The Gates of the Kingdom Book Series

The Little Gate of the Great King

by Colin Baker

Part 1

...And God said, Let the earth sprout tender sprouts, the plant seeding seed, the fruit tree producing fruit according to its kind, whichever seed is in it on the earth. And it was so. And the earth bore tender sprouts, the plant seeding seed according to its kind, and the fruit tree producing fruit according to its kind, whichever seed is in it. And God saw that it was good...

And God said, Let the waters swarm with swarmers having a soul of life; and let the birds fly over the earth, on the face of the expanse of the heavens. And God created the great sea animals, and all that creeps, having a living soul, which swarmed the waters, according to its kind; and every bird with wing according to its kind. And God saw that it was good. And God blessed them, saying, Be fruitful and multiply, and fill the waters in the seas; and let the birds multiply in the earth...

And God said, Let the earth bring forth the soul of life according to its kind: cattle, and creepers, and its beasts of the earth, according to its kind. And it was so. And God made the beasts of the earth according to its kind, and cattle according to its kind, and all creepers of the ground according to its kind. And God saw that it was good.

And God said, let Us make man in Our image, according to Our likeness; and let them rule over the fish of the sea, and over the birds of the heavens, and over the cattle, and over all the earth, and over all the creepers creeping on the earth. And God created the man in His own image; in the image of God He created him. He created them male and female. And God blessed them; and God said to them, Be fruitful and multiply, and fill the earth, and subdue it, and rule over the fish of the seas, and over birds of the heavens, and over all beasts creeping on the earth…

And God saw everything that He had made and behold, it was very good. (Genesis 1:11-31 extracts LITV)

"For the earth will be filled with the knowledge of the glory of the Lord, as the waters cover the sea." (Habakkuk 2:14 NASU)

Every seed that sprouts, every flower bud that opens, every bird that sings, gives testimony to the fact that God's desire is fulfilled in it …to his glory! And in that glory they exult with their Creator …full of life. Together their spirits are ascendant as they dance the dance of the double helix; the dance of life …

"Ahh …the lot falls to Z'kharyah! So be it 'ah (brothers). Adonai has chosen. Z'kharyah shall offer up the 'Shemoneh Esrei' with incense before Adonai."

A rumble of agreement rolls around the circle, and the Priests of Abijah disburse, leaving one aged priest staring at the lot with a questioning look in his eyes.

It had been a very long time since he had been chosen …A time of deep perplexity and of crying out to God, the Father of all.

Zechariah's deep longing; his ceaseless prayer to father a son was somewhat raw after keeping the recent fast. Hope itself had long since died in him, but each time God moved in his life, something stirred deep inside and brought a tear to his weary eyes. Still; he dared not hope.

When the time came, he found that there were more people praying in the courtyard than usual and even the court of the women was full. This did not surprise the aged priest one little bit. He knew that the people had come to cry out to God for relief from their oppressors …and from the lawlessness that pervaded Judea.

They trusted that on this day he would smell the fragrant incense offered, and hear their cry …and maybe even answer their prayer. It was all they could do. There was no other hope. All other hope had been dashed by the sword until hope itself had almost died. But deep inside, something still embraced a hope in God …Age old promises of a deliverer who would come from God himself to redeem his people; Israel, and set them free … The Messiah!

He approached the doorway to the inner court…

Having entered into the sanctuary alone, he takes the burning incense and places it upon that small golden altar which stood before the curtain …and begins to pray the 'Shemoneh Esrei', as was the custom …

> "Blessed are you, Adonai Eloheinu, God of 'avoteinu (our fathers), Elohei Avraham, Elohei Yitzchak vElohei Ya'akov, the great, mighty and revered El 'Elyon, who gives kindnesses plentiful, the creator of all, who recalls the good deeds of the 'avot and who brings a Redeemer to their children's children for his name's sake, in love. O king, helper, saviour and shield. Blessed are you Adonai, the shield of Avraham."

> "You, Adonai, are mighty forever. You are the reviver of the dead. You are greatly able to save. You cause the wind to blow and the rain to fall. You sustain the living in

loving-kindness. You revive the dead with great compassion.

You support the falling, heal the sick, set free the bound and keep faith with those who sleep in the dust. Who is like you O master of mighty deeds? Who compares to you, a king who puts to death and restores to life, and brings forth salvation?"

"...Return us 'Avinu, to your Torah; draw us near, our King, to serve you. Restore us to your presence in complete repentance. Blessed are you Adonai ...you desire repentance."

"Forgive us 'Avinu, for we have sinned; pardon us, our King, for we have rebelled ... Blessed are you Adonai, the gracious one, who abundantly forgives."

"Behold our affliction and champion our cause, and redeem us speedily for the sake of thy Name. Blessed are you, Adonai, Redeemer of Yisra'el."

"Heal us Adonai, and we shall be healed; save us and we will be saved, for you are the one we praise. Bring complete healing for all our sicknesses. May it be your will, Adonai Elohei, Elohei 'Avoteinu, that you send complete healing from Heaven to Elisheva, along with all others who suffer in Yisra'el, for you are our faithful and compassionate Healer and King. Blessed are you, Adonai, Our Healer."

"Sound the great shofar for our freedom, and raise a banner to gather our exiles ... Blessed are you Adonai, who re-gathers the scattered of his people, Yisra'el."

"...And may you establish the throne of David in Yerushalayim without delay. Blessed are you Adonai, the Builder of Yerushalayim."

"May the seed of thy servant David flourish without delay and may you exult in your salvation. For in your salvation we hope all the day. Blessed are you Adonai, who brings forth the Horn of our salvation."

"...Blessed are you Adonai, who restores his presence to Tziyon."

"...You are the Rock and Shield of our salvation, you alone from generation to generation ... Every day your miracles are with us; your wonders and favours always, evening, morning, and afternoon. We put our hope in you. For all these things we bless and exult your Name, our King, without ceasing. And all the living shall confess you forever and praise your Name in truth, O God of our salvation and our help forever! Blessed are you Adonai,

'The Good One' is your Name. To you it is right to give thanks."

"Grant peace, blessing, goodness, grace, kindness and compassion upon us and upon all your people Yisra'el. Bless us 'Avinu, all of us as one, with the light of your face, for with the light of your face you gave to us, Adonai Eloheinu, the Torah of life and love …of kindness, righteousness, blessing, compassion, life and peace. Blessed are you Adonai, who blesses his people Yisra'el with shalom."

As is the custom of the Priests, Zechariah turns to his left, bows, and prays: "He who makes peace in his heights…" then turning back, he bows forward towards the incense altar, the curtain and the presence beyond, and prays: "May he make shalom upon us…" then straightening his aged back: "and upon all Yisra'el …Amen."

As he opens his eyes …light! There! Right in front of him! To the right of the altar! Stands a mighty angel of God! Startled and terrified at the sight, the old man almost falls over backwards.

"Don't be afraid Z'kharyah. Your prayer has been heard. Your wife, Elisheva, will bear you a son. You shall name him Yochanan. He will be a great joy to you and your delight will be in him. Many people will rejoice when he is born because he will be great in the sight of Adonai."

"He is never to drink wine or any other liquor."

"He will be filled with the Ruach HaKodesh, even from his mother's womb."

"He will turn many of the people of Isra'el to their God."

"He will go ahead of Adonai in the spirit and power of Eliyahu, to turn the hearts of the 'avot to their ben, and the disobedient to the wisdom of the righteous; to prepare a people for Adonai."

"By w what can I b be sh shore of th th this. I I am an old m m man. My w wife; sh she is w well on in y years?"

"I am Gavri'el! I stand in the presence of Y'haveh! I was sent! …to speak to you; to give you this good news. What I have said will be fulfilled in its season, but because you didn't believe my words, you will be silent. You will be completely incapable of speech until these things take place."

Six months later, at the time of the Feast of the Dedication, in Nazareth – Galilee of the Gentiles – Mary retires to her room for the night.

She cherishes the joy they have just shared together around the meal table …Her father's telling of all the favourite stories of the Maccabee liberation and the dedication of God's Temple.

She cherishes the warmth of hope that was kindled in them as her mother lit the memorial candles. It was a tradition with her people that a woman should bring the light into the home on such occasions.

For Mary, there is one more light of hope to be lit each night before she goes to bed. After tucking in her little sister, she takes a small oil lamp from its place on the window sill, bounces down the stairs, and pours in a little oil to the broad grins and knowing smiles of her kin who are still sitting around the table telling stories and sharing in the wine. With hardly a hint of embarrassment, she goes to the table, lights the lamp off the festive candle, and skips back up the stairs, knowing full well the laughter and comment she has aroused in the guests.

She places the small lamp in the window, as she has done every night since her betrothal to Yosef at Tabernacles two long months before. It is a sign to her bridegroom that she is ready …but tonight, more than that, it is a sign of an undying hope in her people; a hope of salvation, and a hope where joy resides when all around is darkness and gloom.

In stark contrast to the warm glow of their home, the night beyond her window was dark … even the moon was dimmed by cloud. She knew it would rain before morning and she was not fond of rainy nights.

Mary lay down, but not really for sleep. The loft was warm and it felt good to put her feet up. She could hear the rowdy voices of Uncle Ammon and her father downstairs as the wine loosened their tongues just a little more than usual. They were both very reserved men on any normal day.

She knew that Yosef would not come for her that night. Apart from the rain, she had seen him that very afternoon, and it was a custom for the groom not to see his bride for at least a week before the marriage. In some ways she had been disappointed to see him, but glad at the same time. Still, she chose to place the candle in the window. It was special to her, and it had become a witness also between her and Adonai. Each night she placed it with a prayer for Yosef and herself, and for her people.

It was long after the last voices had departed the gate, the air had chilled, and the front door latch finally dropped that she felt ready for sleep.

Suddenly, she sensed a strange light in the room, as if the moon was shining brightly through the window. Startled, she turned and sat up. There, beside her lamp, stood an angel …shining with the glory of God!

Gabriel approached closer. Mary braced herself and swung her feet to the floor, but was too afraid to rise before such an awesome being of light…

"Shalom, recipient of surrounding grace! Adonai is with you! You are blessed among women!"

"Don't be afraid Miryam, for you have found favour with Ha'Elyon. Behold; you will conceive in your womb and bear a son! You shall name him Yeshua. He will be great, and will be called Ben-Ha'Elyon. Adonai Elohim will give him the throne of his father, David, and he will rule over the house of Ya'akov to the ages. His Kingdom shall never end!"

"How shall this happen?! I am a virgin!"

"The Ruach HaKodesh will come upon you, and the power of Ha'Elyon will overshadow you …So the holy child born to you will be called Ben-Elohim."

"Your doda, Elisheva, who is advanced in years – everyone says she is barren – she has conceived a son, and is six months pregnant. With Y'haveh, nothing is impossible!"

Bowing at the Name, Mary responds out of heartfelt adoration and fear of her God…

"Behold, I am the bondservant of Adonai. May it be done to me as you have said."

With those simple words, on this night, Mary has 'dedicated her temple'.

Gabriel turns, and in the blink of an eye, he is gone.

Mary will never be the same again. She has committed herself to the 'non-impossible'!

She is not sure how she managed to say such words, and incredulously ponders the sound of her own voice saying what she said!

One thing she knows for sure; she must see Elisheva straight away.

❊ ❊ ❊ ❊ ❊

www.colininthespirit.com

The Little Gate of the Great King

Part 2

As they prepare breakfast, Mary and her mother, find themselves alone. The men are a little late in rising. She decides to take the chance…

"'Em?" ("Mother?")

"Yes, Precious … What troubles you?"

"Oh, nothing really, I was just wondering about Doda Elisheva (Beloved Relative Elizabeth). We haven't seen her in a long time. Have you heard any news of her lately?"

Mary's mother covers the jar of goat's milk she was about to pour and looks very thoughtfully at Mary…

"Elisheva and Z'kharyah are at home at their house in the hill country. Your dod has lost his voice and I've heard that Elisheva is not well either."

"Not well? Is that all? She might be very sick! What if she's dying? She could be dying and we wouldn't even know about it!"

"Oh Miryam, don't be silly. If she were dying, someone would have told us. None of the guests said anything about the matter last night. Why are you so concerned about your doda, Elisheva, all of a sudden?"

"'Imi (my mother)!? We should all be concerned if she's not well."

"Yosef is going that way tomorrow. He has some work to do out there. I thought it might be nice if I paid her a visit. That way I could bring back news of how she really is."

"Ahh-ha! So, that's what you're up to! I knew there'd be something like that going on."

"Miryam; it's raining, and the roads are a mess. What makes you think your 'av is going to let you go out in such conditions?"

"'Em, I just thought we could talk about it. It's a matter of trust really."

"You know full well that we trust you …and Joseph. That's not the point! What about other people who see you gallivanting about the countryside together? It's just not on!"

Just then, Mary's father comes in, lays aside his walking stick, and sits down at the table…

"What's not on? Is there something going on here that I should know about?"

"Oh, 'Avi (my father); it's Elisheva… She's not well and I just want to go and visit her. Please, 'Avi!!!"

"It's raining."

"Not now 'Avi; tomorrow … Yosef is going that way. I could go with him, and 'ahoti (my sister) could be chaperone."

"And what makes you think it won't be raining tomorrow young lady?"

"So, I can go then, if the sun is shining?!"

"Miryam, it has rained every morning for the last week. But if you insist, then you can go if the sun shines in the morning …only if the sun shines … and no arguments. I don't want to hear anything more about the matter."

"Oh, thank you 'Avi!" exclaims Mary, leaping up to kiss her father, planting a smile on his face that meets with quite a different kind of look from his wife…

"It will rain. Don't worry woman!"

That night by the lamp, Mary makes two requests of her Lord: forgiveness for misleading her parents, and sunshine in the morning. Both requests are granted. She is the recipient of surrounding grace.

The next day the two Marys walk out into brilliant morning light to break the news to Joseph about their journey into the hill country to visit Elizabeth, leaving their mum and dad to sort out their little differences at home.

Late afternoon finds them in the courtyard of Zechariah, who had been sitting with his nephew, the son of Hezir, making a shopping list of sorts on a slate. Joseph sits down with the men, while Mary goes in to Elizabeth and her sister goes with Salome, their cousin's wife, to the kitchen.

When Elizabeth heard Mary's greeting, the baby in her womb leapt and she was filled with the Holy Spirit. She cried out: "Of all women, you are being blessed. How blessed is the child in your womb!"

"But who am I that v'em Adoni (the mother of my Lord) should come to me? As soon as I heard the sound of your voice, the baby in my womb leapt for joy!"

"Blessed is she believing. All those things told her by Adonai will be fulfilled!"

At Elizabeth's embrace, reality strikes home and Mary, filled with the Holy Spirit, cries out:

> "My soul magnifies Adonai, and my spirit rejoices in 'El Yesa'i (God my Savior), for he looked upon the humble state of his

servant-girl. Just imagine; from now on, all generations will call me blessed!"

"Elohim has done great things for me. Holy is his name!"

"His mercy is to generations of generations of those who fear him!"

"He has performed mighty deeds with his arm and routed the secretly proud."

"He brought down rulers from their thrones and exulted the humble."

"He filled the hungry with good things and sent the rich away empty."

"He has helped his servant Isra'el, never forgetting the mercy, which he promised to 'avoteinu …to Avraham, and to his seed forever!"

We assume it fell to Joseph to take little Mary and 'an explanation' back to his father in law. Mary had decided to stay on with Elizabeth for what turned out to be three whole months …so magnetic was the bond between them, and so insistent was Elizabeth that she should stay.

After Mary had returned home, the time came for Elizabeth to give birth, and she gave birth to a son.

Her neighbors and relatives all rejoiced with her when they heard what great mercy the Lord had displayed toward her.

On the eighth day, when they came to circumcise the child, they were going to call him Zacharias after his father. But Elizabeth said, "No. He must be called Yochanan!" And they said to her, "None of your dod are called by that name."

And they made signs to his father about what he wanted him called. He asked for a tablet and wrote: "His name is Yochanan." And they were all astonished.

At once, Zechariah's power of speech returned and he began to speak in praise of God.

Fear came on all those living around them, and all these matters were being talked about in all the hill country of Judea. All who heard them kept them in mind, saying, "What then will this child become? For the hand of the Lord was certainly with him."

And his father Zechariah was filled with the Holy Spirit, and prophesied:

> "Praised be Adonai, the Elohim of Yisra'el,
>
> for he has visited us and made a ransom to liberate his people.

He has raised up a horn of salvation for us in the house of his servant, David.

It is just as he said by the mouth of his holy prophets from the beginning;

Salvation from our enemies, and from the hand of all who hate us;

to show mercy toward our 'av, and to remember his holy covenant;

the oath which he swore to Avraham avinu.

To grant us that we, being rescued from the hand of our enemies, might serve him without fear, in holiness and righteousness before him all our days!

And you, child, will be called the prophet of Ha'Elyon;

for you will go before Adonai to prepare his ways…

To give his people the knowledge of salvation by the forgiveness of their sins,

because of the tender mercy of Eloheinu, with which the Sunrise from Heaven will visit us,

to shine upon those who sit in darkness and the shadow of death…

to guide our feet into the way of peace."

The child grew and became strong in spirit and lived in the desert until the day of his public appearance to Israel.

Mary arrives home less than a week before John's birth and the 'Festival of Spring'; Passover …

"Oh, Bati (my daughter), we've missed you so much!" Mary and her mother embrace as if they had been apart for years…

"My, but you look well. Your face is more beautiful to my eyes than ever I can remember!"

"Oh 'Imi; really … It's only been a few short months!"

"Short for you maybe, but your 'av and I have been so worried for you."

"I am perfectly alright 'Em. Didn't Yosef give you my message?"

"Yes, of course, but we just didn't expect you to be gone so long. How is your doda?"

"She is perfectly alright. She's having a baby."

"Yes, I gathered that from the message Yosef brought back. So it's really true then?"

"Yes. It will be any day now, perhaps even today. Salome is with her even now to deliver."

"That's amazing! They are too old …Both of them."

"With Adonai, 'Imi, nothing is impossible."

Just then, Mary's father hobbles out from the house…

"Miryam; Bati! You're just in time to help with preparations for Pesach. We've invited the neighbors to join us as Barukh and your 'ah have gone up to Yerushalayim for the feast. Today I must bring home a lamb …and the house is not yet set in order."

"I will bring the lamb 'avi."

"It's not far," he says, leaning on his staff.

"You can take your 'ahot with you. It's in the manger behind the house of Salmai. But later; come … tell us all the news of Z'kharyah and Elisheva. We got this strange story from Yosef…"

"'Avi; it's true …They're having a son!"

"Oh, a son now is it?! How can you be so sure it will be a boy?"

"The angel, Gavri'el, appeared to Z'kharyah in the Temple and told him so before the child was even conceived!"

Mary's heart was pounding. Would she dare tell her father everything?

"Who told you this?"

"Doda Elisheva told me herself. She even showed me Z'kharyah's drawing of Gavri'el."

"Well, it certainly is a miracle. They've been childless for as long as I can remember."

"Your stay with them certainly hasn't done you any harm. You're looking absolutely glorious. They must have fed you on milk and honey, did they?"

"'Avi; Adonai has surrounded me with his grace…"

"That, my little sweetheart, is plain to see. You'd better rest up a bit before you go to Salmai's for the lamb. I hope you won't have to carry it."

"That's alright 'Avi. I don't mind carrying a little lamb."

"That's alright 'Avi. I don't mind carrying a little lamb."

That afternoon, Mary carries in a perfect little lamb, freshly cleaned and lovingly dried with a towel. With a loving kiss, she places it in the living room, and sits down beside it for comfort as it adjusts to its new surrounds.

"I will call you 'Anwa, (meekness) for you are the meekest little lamb I have ever met."

"'Imi; what are you cooking? It smells wonderful!"

"I'm baking bread … Some for us, and some to sell at the market in the morning. Your 'av says it's better than selling the surplus chametz (yeast) to some Gentile for half price. Only four days now to Erev Pesach you know."

"Yes … I know," says Mary, hugging ''Anwa' to her cheek as tears begin to well up in her eyes.

Her mother, hearing Mary's silence, closes the oven and walks in…

"You never learn, do you girl."

"Miryam; you're a betrothed woman now. You must learn to restrain yourself for the sake of custom …and you should not be sitting like that on the floor either."

"Yes 'Imi. I just can't help the way I feel. Are we not meant to feel remorse for the life of the lamb? Is its life not forfeit in place of ours?"

"Oh Bati, sometimes I wonder why I even bother trying. Come and help me knead the last batch of dough. Be careful not to spill any yeast. It will not go unnoticed by your 'av you know."

Mary's rising, just a little slower than usual, is glanced by her mother out of the corner of her eye as she returns to the kitchen…

"You must be feeling tired. It's been a big day for you."

"Yes. It was an early start, and such a long walk. I've been feeling like just going to bed all afternoon."

"Well, this won't take long …then you might have time for a short nap before supper."

That evening, Mary slept so soundly that her mother could not wake her at supper time. This and many other little things known only to watchful mothers caused her to become … more than concerned … perhaps even a little 'suspicious', of Mary's state. But it was Pesach (Passover) …so, in the words of her husband, 'all such matters shall therefore be set aside until after the final day of observance is complete.'

Three mornings later, Mary is not feeling well. After barely tasting her breakfast, she returns to her room, for she knows that 'Anwa will be slain. She does not want to see it, yet the images of red blood on white wool are vivid in her memory from Passovers gone by.

In the afternoon, as she helps her mother prepare the Seder (Passover meal), she tries to put it out of her mind …but of course, on such an occasion as this, this is just impossible.

As evening approaches, it is time for 'Bedikat Chametz'; the search for the leaven. This they do every year throughout the house under the supervision of Mary's father, who also pronounces the blessing. Her mother holds a candle, Mary, a wooden spoon and her little sister wields a feather. Together, the four of them begin to search every corner…

"Blessed are you Adonai Eloheinu, who has set us apart with his commandments, and commanded us to remove the Chametz."

As they search together, Mary's father breaks the customary silence to just drop a comment:

"You know Miryam, chametz is really just a sign. It speaks of the evil impulses of the heart which arouse people to do evil deeds. When we search for the chametz, we should really search our own deeds and hearts."

"Yes 'Avi, you have taught us this from an early age. Why do you remind me again now?"

Mary's mother looks up, and is about to respond, but Heli, resting one hand on her mother's shoulder, replies; "Adonai has commanded that we should teach his precepts to our children and to our children's children. This is why I never grow tired of explaining to you the story." But in the light of the candle, Mary can see in her mother's eyes that she knows.

Mary feels feint, yet they continue the search, carefully checking every part of the house. In the end, they have half a spoonful of crumbs and one piece of crust.

The crumbs, the spoon, the candle and the crust all go into a bag to be burned.

Heli, looking at Mary, pronounces his usual disclaimer:

"All chametz which is in my house, which I have not found, and of which I am unaware shall be considered void and ownerless, like the dust of the earth!"

A knock at the door says that the neighbours have arrived. Her parents greet the guests, and Mary, holding back tears, busies herself with laying the rugs and cushions around the table. It is time to begin the Seder.

The atmosphere is lively, and Mary finds relief from her fears in the company of the guests.

Her mother slips out to the kitchen, returning with a small lamp. Everyone turns to watch her bringing the light, as a woman does on nights such as this.

She carefully lights the candles, then placing the lamp on the table, she covers her eyes with her hands as is the custom, and pronounces the blessing:

"Blessed are you Adonai Eloheinu, King of the universe, who has set us apart by his Torah, and in whose name we light the festival lights."

As she removes her hand, she wipes a tear; something entirely foreign to the traditions of that night …and then fixes it with a smile.

Raising an eyebrow and nodding to Mary, her father gives the signal to pour the first cup…

Sitting up, he reminds them of the cup and pronounces the blessing:

> "Therefore, say to the ben-Yisra'el, I am Adonai, and I will bring you out from under the burdens of Misrayim, and will deliver you from their slavery. And I will redeem you with an outstretched arm and with great judgments."

> "Blessed are you, Adonai Eloheinu, king of the universe, creator of the fruit of the vine."

> "Blessed are you, Adonai; you hallow the festive seasons."

"Amen! Amen!" comes the chorus of response as they all drink the cup of 'the bringing out from'; 'the cup of the setting apart'.

Mary brings the water, towel over one arm. She pours it carefully over the hands of each into a bowl; beginning with her father, then the guests as was their custom…

Taking a sprig of fresh parsley, Heli exhorts the family: "Let us dip the karpaz in salt water and be reminded of the new life that came out of the suffering in Misrayim."

Dipping, they all pronounce the blessing:

> "Blessed are you, Adonai Eloheinu, king of the universe, creator of the fruit of the ground.

Mary's mother gets up and brings the matzah, the maror (bitter herb dip) and the haroset. Mary pours the wine; the second cup; 'the cup of redemption'…

> "…And the blood shall be a sign to you on your houses. I will see the blood, and I will pass over you. You shall not be touched when I strike the land of Misrayim (Two Kingdoms; Egypt). And the day shall be a memorial for you. You shall celebrate it as a feast to Adonai, for all your generations. You shall

celebrate it as a law forever. Blessed are you, Adonai Eloheinu, King of the universe, creator of the fruit of the vine."

"Amen! Amen!"

After the wine, when the conversation finds a lull, at a nod from her father, Mary once more washes the hands of the guests with bowl and pitcher and towel… Heli, taking the matzah; blessing, he breaks it …passing it around at the "Amen".

After the matzah, Mary and her mother bring the pesah; the whole roast lamb …and place it on the table.

To the hungry souls reclining there, the aroma of satisfaction is overwhelming.

Together they all pronounce the blessing:

"Blessed are you, Adonai Eloheinu, king of the universe, who set us apart by your commandments and commanded us to eat the pesah."

The feast begins with a cheer and laughter. Mary immediately begins to refill everyone's cup…

Their neighbour, Sarai, compliments her on her appearance:

"My, but you are looking beautiful tonight Miryam. Your stay with your doda didn't do you any harm, did it! I do believe you've even put on a little weight since you've been away."

Embarrassed, Mary glances across to her mother, who has obviously been listening, for their eyes meet. Looking back to Sarai, she finds her glancing at her mother. It is too much for Mary. She places the wine down, turns, and to the bewilderment of the guests, runs up the stairs; crying, leaving them to question each other and apologize to their hearts content.

Mary's mother begins to rise up, but Heli restrains her...

"Later, wife; give her time to settle down. Pesach is a festive occasion. It is holy to Adonai."

Baruch's daughter, who is around the same age as Mary, gets up... "I'll go," she says, heading for the stairs.

At the end of the meal, after the table had been mostly cleared and her mother was washing the hands, Mary and Elisha come back down the stairs and take their places at the table...

"We saved you girls some lamb. We will wait for you to eat before we all drink from the 'Cup of Redemption'."

"The Lamb is in my heart, 'Avi, and I'm already satisfied …but I will eat just a little if it pleases you that I should eat."

*"The Lamb is in my heart, 'Avi, and
I'm already satisfied."*

"…If it pleases me?! Adonai, blessed be his name, has commanded that we should eat!"

She takes a morsel, dips it, and swallows hard, but she cannot get the images of red on white out of her mind. Her friend, Elisha, has no such problem.

The silence at the table is stifling. Elisha's mother takes up the towel and the bowl for the two girls, and Heli continues by quoting a scripture that had been fresh on his mind that day:

> "In the words of the prophet, Mal'akhi: 'Remember the Torah of Moshe my servant, which I commanded him in Horev for all Yisra'el.' Adonai, blessed be his name, also said at that time: 'Look, I am sending you Eliyahu the prophet, before the coming of the great and terrible day of Adonai. He shall turn the hearts of the 'av to their ben, and the hearts of the ben to their 'av, that I not come and strike the land with utter destruction."

Heli sits up…

"Come; let us say the blessing together."

> "Blessed be HaShem from this time forth and forever!"

Heli leads on…

"Let us bless Eloheinu, of whose food we have eaten, and through whose goodness we live."

> "Blessed be Eloheinu, of whose food we have eaten, and by whose goodness we live!"

Taking the cup, Heli finishes…

> "Blessed are you, Adonai Eloheinu, king of the universe, who in mercy and compassion gives bread to all flesh; for your mercy is everlasting. May food never fail us, for your great name's sake."

> "Blessed are you, Adonai, who feeds and sustains all, and does good to all. We thank you because you brought us from the land of Misrayim, out of the house of slaves, to a good land; we thank you for your life, grace and mercy. We thank you at all times, forever. As it is said: 'When you have eaten and are satisfied, praise Adonai Eloheinu for the good land he has given you. Blessed are you, Adonai, for the land and for the food."

"Blessed are you Adonai Eloheinu, King of the universe, creator of the fruit of the vine."

"Amen! Amen!"

Heli drinks of 'Redemption', and passes his cup around for all to share.

Mary's mother immediately begins filling the fourth cup; the 'Cup of Acceptance'. When she finally gets to Mary, there are tears in her eyes. She wraps a comforting arm around her daughter as she pours the cup, then, as is the custom, her daughter pours for her. Her hand trembles as Mary pours the wine. Mary steadies it with a touch, and they embrace, cups in hand, bringing a warm response from the guests.

Mary and her mother recline together and everyone places their cup on the table while Heli chants the 'Hallel', stirring them to respond in place along the way as was his custom…

"Servants of Adonai, give praise! Give praise to the name of Adonai! Blessed be the name of Adonai from this moment on and forever!"

He raises the poor from the dust, lifts the needy from the rubbish heap, in order to give him a place among princes, among the princes of his people.

He causes the childless woman to live at home happily as a mother of children.

Tremble, earth, at the presence of the Lord, at the presence of the God of Ya'akov, who turned the rock into a pool of water, flint into flowing spring.

I will call on him as long as I live.

The chords of death were all around me, Sh'ol's constrictions held me fast; I was finding only distress and anguish.

But I called on the name of Adonai; "Please, Adonai! Save me!"

How can I repay Adonai for all his generous dealings with me?

I will raise the cup of salvation and call on the name of Adonai…

Oh, Adonai! I am your slave; I am your slave, the son of your slave-girl; you have removed my fetters.

I will offer a sacrifice of thanks to you and I will call on the name of Adonai.

Praise Adonai, all you nations!

Worship him, all you peoples!

> For his grace has overcome us, and Adonai's truth continues forever.
>
> Yah is my strength and my song, and he has become my salvation.
>
> I will not die; no, I will live and proclaim the great deeds of Yah!
>
> The very rock that the builders rejected has become the cornerstone!
>
> Blessed is he who comes in the name of Adonai…"

(CJB Hallel Extracts)

With cup in hand, Heli pronounces the benediction:

> "Blessed are you, Adonai Eloheinu, king of the universe, who redeemed us and redeemed 'avoteinu from Misrayim ."
>
> "Blessed are you, Adonai Eloheinu, King of the universe, creator of the fruit of the vine."

"Amen! Amen!"

…And so ended the Pesach Seder that year for the houses of Heli and Baruch in Nazareth of Galilee.

"...when ...Mary had been betrothed to Joseph, before they came together she was found to be with child..." (Matthew 1:18 Extract NASU)

* * * * *

www.colininthespirit.com

The Little Gate of the Great King

Part 3

…And so the rumour spread in Nazareth in those days which would one day come back to the ears of the One hidden that night in Mary's womb. It would prompt unspoken thoughts in many minds and the vehement accusation lying implicitly obvious in the words of the Pharisees: "Where is your father?! We are not illegitimate children; we have one father; God himself!"

Of course, to Joseph's ears, the news he heard from his father, Jacob, was absolutely devastating. But God did not leave him in his anguish. Mary's prayers by the lamp at her window each night brought him into that surrounding grace which was covering her.

God sent Joseph an angel in a dream, saying, 'Joseph, son of David, do not be afraid to take Mary as your wife. For that which is in her is generated by the Holy Spirit. She will bear a son, and you shall call His name Jesus, for He shall save His people from their sins.

All this happened to fulfil that which was spoken by the Lord through the prophet, saying,

Behold! …The virgin will conceive and will bear a son, and they will call His name Emmanuel; 'God with us'.'

Late that very night, Joseph did as the angel of the Lord commanded him. He came for his wife, and found the lamp still burning in the window, and his virgin bride ready for his coming …yet with child.

Shavuot (Pentecost) came and went like a shadow for Mary, who kept away from the public eye, just as Elizabeth had done. Her relationship with Joseph flourished, for it was entirely built upon believing. They believed one another because they believed God, and because of the Name. Gabriel had given to them both the same name …the name; 'Yeshua'.

And so their love grew and grew without any union in the flesh. Joseph just put such thoughts out of his mind, for the presence of the Lord had made them to vanish.

One evening, after the meal, Joseph is reclining, his head upon Mary's lap, his right foot upon his left knee. Mary is combing the sawdust out of his hair…

"Those Romans are painful. They ordered two more sets of stocks today, but the price they pay is less than what the timber is worth let alone the work I must do on it. If it weren't for the timber I salvaged off Shaarim's old barn, I'd be working for less than nothing!"

"That's alright though. The new door for the synagogue will fetch a better rate. I went and measured it up today. El'azar says that the Romans are holding a census; something to do with Augusts' birthday. They're sending a special Legate to oversee the whole of Syria. There's so much trouble in the land, Saturnius is apparently hard pressed just enforcing his rule."

"When will this be?"

"I'm not sure. El'azar said that the Sanhedrin would almost certainly advise the new Hegemon when he arrives, to send everyone to the towns of their 'avot …That's where they keep all the ancestral records you know."

"El'azar was in a bit of a fluster about getting the records for Natzeret up to date. I think it also explains the new door. They want to admit people one at a time for the census.

"You will have to go to Beit-Lekhem!"

"It's possible. We'll wait and see."

"Will I have to register too?"

"As far as I know. El'azar said; everybody. Don't worry. I won't leave you behind."

"There is one small detail you should try not to forget about my love."

"Oh... What's that?"

"Just look at me Yosef!"

Joseph cracks a mischievous grin... "I was only joking." he says, knowing that some swift reaction would surely follow.

"'Plenty of midwives in Natzaret,' you say! Yosef; I want Salome. I want to see her before Shavat. I won't be going anywhere without Salome."

"Consider it done my dove. If I'm late home tomorrow, you know where I'll be. I must still rough out those stocks you know."

"Good. At last we're together on this. Now I just wish I could go with you. Make sure you give my love to Elisheva and Z'kharyah ...And bring me back news of baby Yochanan."

"Yes, I would like to see what manner of child is announced by an angel; Gavri'el, no less! And I am very interested in that drawing of Z'kharyah's."

"You're not supposed to know about that, don't forget."

"Don't worry, I will be discrete."

As it turned out, the governor for the census, one Publius Sulpicius Quirinus, acting on advice from the Sanhedrin, set the registration for Bethlehem right on the date that Mary was due.

The news looked very grim for anyone who failed to register for such failure implied a refusal of allegiance to Augustus …and to Rome.

It took them over a week to get there, with Salome's concern obviously mounting all the way. They finally arrived on the very last morning for registration. They went straight to the synagogue to register.

All afternoon they tried their relatives for a place to stay, but in the end, they found that there was not even room for them at the inn!

The Feast of Trumpets was about to begin just a short walk away in Jerusalem, and, apart from the census, Bethlehem had always absorbed the overflow from the feasts. Every last option was full, except for one; the manger …The manger of Bethlehem.

One ram and seven perfect yearling lambs had just vacated the premises, heading up to Jerusalem for the Feast. The rest of the 'Sacrificial Flock' were out in the fields that afternoon. And so it was that a place was made for the Little Lamb of God to enter this dark world.

Joseph shoveled and swept out the dung, made a bed for Mary from the left-over straw, and Salome cleaned and lined a feeding trough. Together, they carried it in and placed it alongside of Mary, for the birth pains had already begun.

Salome prepared the swaddling cloth and busied herself with all the preparations of a skilled midwife. Joseph had no idea what to do. When the waters burst, there was blood!

When the waters burst, there was blood!

At just a look from Salome, Joseph headed for the door, his head spinning.

He sat down, breathing deep the fresh evening air, listening to Mary's pain.

When he looked up, the sun was just dipping into the haze of the horizon. Some stars and the new moon had become visible in the west. There was something mesmerizing about the scene…

Suddenly; the sound of a shofars; Rosh Hashanah …the New Year had just begun!

Looking north, he could see the glow of the great signal fire on the Mount of Olives. He remembered how every year it lit up the east gate and the temple on this night.

From the walls of that city, and in the temple itself, trumpets would be sounding into the night, as if to herald the coming of a great king, for this was their custom ...a commandment from God Himself. It made him wonder at the place he stood, for this very night celebrated not only the birth of his forefather, Isaac, but also that day when God created Adam. According to the traditions of his forefathers, not only his own people, but the whole race of man was begotten of God on this day. 'What manner of child was this breaking out from Mary's womb?'

...the whole race of man was begotten of God on this day. 'What manner of child was this breaking out from Mary's womb?'

The thought floated across his mind "...and the best you could provide was a manger!" until he remembered God's sovereignty.

* * * * *

That signal fire was but the first in a chain that skipped across to Mount Gilboa on the east, then right across the Desert of Aram to Babylon, where the faithful waited for confirmation to come from

Jerusalem that that thin crescent they could see in the western sky was in fact the new moon; it was officially New Year …and time to sound the shofar…

From the 'Astronomer's Turret' on the wall of Babylon, two magi of the eastern school looked up from that fire into the western sky…

"Anyone can see that it is a new moon tonight. What's the point of that fire my dod?"

"It is for those who cannot tell the times and the seasons my young neked (nephew) …And for dark nights when God hides the heavens from the eyes of men."

"What are you looking at?"

"A virgin."

"Where!?" (The shofars of the synagogues begin to sound throughout the city…)

"I thought that might catch your attention. Look… right there above the moon; Virgo … clothed in the sun, with the moon under her feet. This is a sign that we've been waiting for for many generations …the Virgin gives birth! It's just as Belt'shatzar taught, and this is the very year which he calculated. If it is true, then there will be another sign. We had better call the brothers. This could be awesome."

"Our eyes shall know no sleep tonight. This night, my nekhed, we shall all watch and wait."

"Wait for what? What shall be the second sign?"

"I'll explain later. Run quickly. Tell Aden to sound the gong in the courtyard. All the 'ashshawph must come quickly or they'll miss the sign of the Virgin."

❊ ❊ ❊ ❊ ❊

Between Bethlehem and Jerusalem lies the narrow Plain of the Rephaim. This is the place where the temple flocks are grazed. This night, the shepherds will camp together, for it is a night of celebration; a night for wishing each other the blessing of the New Year…

At dusk they share a meal around the fire, and at the rising of the new moon, they watch for the great signal fire on the mountain. As the stars begin to shine, the golden glow appears. One has a ram's horn. He sounds it into the night air to the cheers of all. Rising up, they each, in turn, embrace, pronouncing the blessing over and over, brother to brother as they go…

> "May you be inscribed in God's book for life eternal. May you behold the beauty of Adonai

and be remembered in his heavenly temple. May you prosper and be blessed with peace."

※ ※ ※ ※ ※

Joseph winced as Mary cried out …Then, the sound of the baby crying. He dashes in…

"Are they alright?!" he blurts out to Salome as she gently wipes the newborn clean.

Gently wrapping the newborn, she replies, "Yes; Look," rising with the child in her arms. Coming close, she passes him to Joseph, who is grinning from ear to ear …and trembling.

Kneeling beside Mary, he brings the new born Son of God beside his mother where they can see him together. Heaven's eyelids open, dark eyes all starry in the soft light of the lamp… He looks around … and grins, revealing dimples that would accompany him all his days.

…And so his first conquest was made; the heart of Joseph, son of David, carpenter of Nazareth. With no resistance, no fear, no hesitation at all, he kisses the Son, handing him to Mary. Taking him in her arms, she does exactly the same thing …and after the conquest; a yawn.

※ ※ ※ ※ ※

Out in the fields, the shepherds return from their rounds of the herds and sit together around the fire…

'"Ah, what a glorious night", says Benjamin, lying flat on his back and gazing up at the stars.

"Yeah, I'd rather be out here on a night like this than back in town …even if it is Rosh Hashanah."

"Yerushalayim'll be a rowdy place t'night. Trumpets, feastin', dancin' even …But you're right, I kind of like these fields too. The stars seem so close t'night, you could just about reach out 'n touch 'em."

"Yeah, and we don't have to dress up and pretend to be someone special neither," adds Neriah. "…Can't imagine you lot dressin' up anyway. Yous wouldn't know what to do in a set a fine clothes. I dressed up only once in my life; for my bar-mitzvah. On that big occasion, 'Avi even made me wear his turb'n," he says, laughter echoing around the fire.

"What is that!" exclaims Benjamin, as everyone looks up toward his gaze.

They all watch frozen and dumbstruck as a brilliant star flares into blinding light …towards them! They are still looking up at where it had been when 'it' arrives.

Glorious light floods their whole field, and right there, beside their lightless burning firewood, an angel of God; awesome in appearance and radiant with glory!

"Do not fear. For behold, I proclaim good news to you; a great joy which will be to all people. Today a Saviour, Adonai Ha Mashiach, was born to you in the city of David. And this shall be a sign to you: You will find a babe, wrapped and lying in the manger."

Suddenly there appeared myriads of heavenly beings, praising God and saying, 'Glory to God in the highest ... peace on earth and good will among men!'

Their rapturous praise went on and on until the shepherds themselves abandoned their fears and joined in with the heavenly host.

When the myriads of light finally vanished from their sight, the brightest of all nights turned to deep blackness. Except for the flames of their fire which had again become visible, they'd have utterly lost all direction. But they didn't care... They were still praising and jumping and hugging one another like men in a dream.

And so it was that the sacrificial flocks were abandoned that night by their shepherds at the coming of the Little Lamb of God.

And so it was that the sacrificial flocks were abandoned that night by their shepherds at the coming of the Little Lamb of God.

They went straight to the manger of Bethlehem, and found the baby, just as the angel said they would.

It was a sight more wondrous even than the myriads, for, although they had seen many births in that manger, these had all been lambs …and now this one who was the Saviour, Adonai Ha Mashiach himself, lying there in a feeding trough on a bed of straw …wrapped in swaddling clothes! The 'Great One', the Saviour; the Messiah … wrapped in swaddling clothes!

They bowed down in adoration and wept for joy. They had seen God's deliverance. It answered to the deepest longings of their hearts as no mighty king on any great and glorious throne could ever do. They were very familiar with 'swaddling clothes', for they had been struggling against their bondages all their lives. Now comes their saviour, overwhelmingly free and full of joy …not in a palace, but in their manger …not ruling aloof from their struggles, but wrapped in the confines of swaddling clothes! …bright eyes, a gorgeous grin and dimples!

Unable to contain their joy, they spread the news all over town. For a season, it became Bethlehem's best kept secret …A child had been born amongst them to rule on David's throne.

Because of the shepherd's report, the elders of Bethlehem were as excited as children at a birthday party. Within a few short days, they would be urging the 'Royal Family' to stay. They would even offer them a house …an offer which Joseph and Mary would gladly accept.

❋ ❋ ❋ ❋ ❋

The observation platform of the 'Astronomer's Turret' is crowded out with all the magi and their apprentices. There is hardly room to move.

Ghina picks his way through the brothers who are sprawled out all over the platform. He notices that some have dropped off to sleep. Most are watching …some talking in hushed tones. Finally he reaches his uncle, Gaspar, who is leaning back against the outer wall…

"Dod …What will this sceptre that shall rise out of Isra'el look like? Will it be a long line of stars, or just a single star?"

"It could be a single star, for the words of the prophecy are that 'a star will come out of Jacob; a sceptre will rise out of Isra'el'."

"The Great Belt'shatzar taught that this king would come from the tribe of Judah, whose symbol is 'aRi, the lion."

"So that's why you're watching the east. Your waiting for 'aRi to rise."

"Should we not tell the brothers … They're searching the whole sky?!"

"My young neked, all the 'ashshawph have received the same teaching. We shall wait and see who shall be first to recognize the sign."

Two older men approach, picking their way along the wall with many eyes following their movement… Balthazar and Melchior are definitely senior among the Magi…

"'Ah, it is almost time." says Balthazar, "Should we not tell the brothers?"

"I'm a bit worried that the bragging may be a bit much to bear if Bashaa, or Apuulluunideeszu, should happen to spot it first."

"Oh no; Heaven forbid …Not Apuulluunideeszu! His turban would become totally inadequate."

"I thought we might just point it out when it begins to become visible."

"Yes. Good idea! Ghina, you had better get our sarat to come over here. Just quietly... Wake the sleeping ones, but don't make a fuss."

Ghina quietly moves about passing the message and all eyes turn to the gathering of apprentices at the wall. Balthazar speaks in hushed tones to about forty young men who immediately all turn to the eastern sky...

"What is the sign beginning to rise? You can just see half of it now. Who can name the sign?"

"It is 'aRi," says Ubar.

"Yes, now watch the feet."

As Leo rises, the most brilliant star appears at his feet. The gasp at the breathtaking spectacle is audible as they all start to point. The words 'Sharu' and 'sceptre' come mingled with the excited gabble breaking the still of the night air.

Apuulluunideeszu steps up on the catapult ramp and makes the announcement: "A great king has been born this night! May history record that it was I, the great Apuulluunideeszu, who first interpreted the sign!"

Ignoring the cheers of Apuulluunideeszu's apprentices, Melchior quietly poses another question...

"What did Belt'shatzar call Sharu?"

Whispers all around fail to produce any answer, and at length, Melchior answers his own question…

"It is called 'Melech', which means king. But it is not just 'Melech'. Watch carefully…"

"There are two stars! They're moving apart!"

More excitement reverberates through the assembled magi. "What does it mean? Are there two kings? Is one Babylonian and the other Roman? Will Babylon separate from Rome? When will these things happen?"

Melchior quietly poses the next question for his apprentices along his well contemplated line of teaching…

"And what is the name given to the star which moves?"

…for a moment; hesitation.

"It is Tzedek! …Righteousness!"

"Yes. Very good Rabi: 'Melech Tzedek; King of Righteousness' …And the prophecy? …Do any of you know the prophecy taught by Belt'shatzar which relates to this sign?"

"…'The sceptre will not depart from Judah, nor the ruler's staff from between his feet, until he comes to whom it belongs and the obedience of the nations is his.'"

"Master; why then does Tzedek appear to be departing from before the feet of 'aRi?"

"I am not sure my son, but if we watch carefully, we may see other signs, for it is yet more than two hours to the sunrise."

"It shall not depart," states Gaspar, the youngest of the three, with an air of confidence.

"But Master Caspar, Tzedek is Jupiter. It never stands still."

"Watch and learn, young sarat of Melchior. Just watch and learn."

Ever so slowly, 'Tzedek' stopped in its track and returned again to 'Melech' between the feet of ''aRi', 'the Lion'. Blazing brightly in union as before, it again proclaimed the King of Righteousness, then appeared to pass on in the opposite direction! This was something that most of the magi had never seen. How could Jupiter turn around and go the other way? Even the elders were gasping in amazement at the sight.

Gasper and Balthazar were quite familiar with the habits of Jupiter, the king of planets, but this declaration in the heavens and the accuracy of Daniel's predictions had them absolutely awestruck.

"I wonder where this King of the Jews will be born," says Balthazar, eyes transfixed on the sight.

"I don't know," replies Melchior, "The Jews are scattered everywhere from here to Alexandria, to Rome, but one thing I do know; this is a very great King above all other kings. The coming of kings is declared on the earth by men with trumpets, as on this night, but what king has ever been declared by the starry host of God in the heavens?!"

> *"...The coming of kings is declared on the earth by men with trumpets, as on this night, but what king has ever been declared by the starry host of God in the heavens?!"*

Jupiter stopped, as if it had heard Melchior's exclamation, and returned for a third union with Regiel. Together, they were so bright; brighter even than before.

This third time at their declaration, 'Melech Tzedek, King of Righteousness', the magi of Babylon all bowed their faces to the ground and paid homage to the King! At the rising of the sun, the sceptre still remained before the feet of 'aRi, the lion …the Lion of Judah!

The excitement of Babylon's magi lasted right through that day, stirred on by the constant sound of shofars proclaiming the New Year …proclaiming the coming of the king.

❈ ❈ ❈ ❈ ❈

www.colininthespirit.com

The Little Gate of the Great King

Part 4

Apart from a place to stay, the elders of Bethlehem had made sure that all the arrangements were in order for their newborn king.

As the eve of the Day of Atonement approached, just before the setting sun issued in the most holy of Sabbaths; the one day of the year when the High Priest would enter into the Holy of Holies to make atonement by blood for the nation …just then did they circumcise him.

There in the Synagogue of Bethlehem, in the presence of his father, of Joseph, the priest and the elders of David's line, the real blood of atonement was seen by human eyes for the very first time! His father's eyes saw much more. They saw the sign of a covenant cut, for it was on this very day so many years before that he had cut with his people, Israel, a covenant on new tablets of stone to replace the ones they had broken. It would be a covenant neither cut in tablets of stone nor ratified with the blood of bulls and goats…

"What name shall be called upon this child?" chants the priest, the circumcision having been completed.

"His name is Yeshua," replies Joseph, quoting words deeply embedded, "for he will save his people from their sins."

The old priest is stunned by a statement that is just too unbelievable to comprehend. Even so, his hands tremble as he gives the awesome child back to 'his father'.

Twenty three days later, it is Sunday morning, and the day of 'the Redemption of the Son'. On this day, Joseph would pay the redemption price of five silver shekels for the firstborn. Acknowledging that Jesus belonged to God, he would 'redeem' his life back to the kinship of the 'Sons of Israel'.

"Yosef?"

"Yes, my dove?"

"Have you ever had the feeling that things are repeating themselves?"

"That depends … What do you mean?"

"The town elders … The way they are insisting on us staying, and the way they are treating us …it's almost the same as that time I went to visit Doda Miryam and she wouldn't let me go."

"Yes, it seems that anyone who recognizes this child never wants to let him go. There is something so captivating about him. I should know. I am his first captive. Yeshua, you have won my heart! Yes you have…" he says, taking him up in his arms. "…You and those gorgeous little dimples. I'm your slave forever, and I also will never let you go. 'Aviha (your father) is so gracious to loan you to me for only five silver shekels. This day is your 'pidyon-ha-ben'. Today I will make you to be as my own."

And so he did … And so, under law, Jesus became 'the carpenter's son' for a season.

Nine days later, it is time for their first walk up to Jerusalem…

After purchasing a pair of young doves in the market to offer for Mary's atonement, they walk across the city and enter the temple courtyard …

"Yosef …this temple …it is so grand …the people …they are all so dressed up …it frightens me."

"Yes, I know. What I can't understand is that the owner of this house chose you for his handmaiden knowing full well how out of place we feel here."

"There are many women here more beautiful than I."

"No my Dove, you are mistaken. There are none."

"Yosef; you are biased."

"Yes. So is Elohim. He has a strong leaning towards people who are after his own heart."

"Look; that old man has fixed his eyes on us and he's coming this way. Do you know him?"

"Not that I recall, but he seems to know us ...or is it the baby?"

"Shalom; Shalom aleikhem! I am Shim'on," says the ancient one, stretching out his hands to receive the child.

"Oh, blessed be Adonai the giver of hayyim," he proclaims with trembling voice, kissing the holy babe on the forehead, holding him up close to see with aged, teary eyes...

"And now my immutable Master, it is time to release your bond-slave in peace according to your word, for my eyes have seen your yeshu'ah which you prepared before the face of all peoples ...A light for revelation to the nations and the glory of your people Yisra'el."

And blessing his incredulous parents, Simeon hands the child back to Mary...

"Behold, this one is destined for the falling and rising of many in Yisra'el and for a miraculous sign whom people will refuse. Moreover, through your soul shall pass a great sword, that the thoughts of many hearts may be revealed."

Just at that moment, a most ancient woman came on the scene …a prophetess named Anna, daughter of Phanuel of the tribe of Asher. She stayed always in the temple grounds, worshipping there night and day with much prayer and fasting. When she saw the child, taking him in her arms, she began thanking and praising God. From that time she never ceased speaking of him to all who were eagerly watching for the redemption of Jerusalem!

❈ ❈ ❈ ❈ ❈

While Joseph is busy establishing a new carpentry business in Bethlehem, the magi of Babylon are studying the stars with great interest. On the 14th of Adar, as the Jews celebrate their deliverance at Purim, another sign appears as Regiel and Jupiter unite again between the feet of Leo. Again at Shavuot, the Feast of Weeks, the same thing happens. Still, they are not sure where this great King of the Jews has been born.

All of Babylon is buzzing with rumours …all kinds of rumours. Caspar, Melchior and Balthazar wait, patiently watching the heavens. Nine months have gone by. It is the evening of the 25th of Sivan…

"'Ahi, will you never grow tired of watching for a sign? Eventually you will have to face the fact that we have missed it. We have no idea where he was born, so how can we possibly go to pay homage before his face?"

"Patience Caspar. The one who set the stars in their courses is not a man that he should be influenced by our impatience."

"So true ahi, yet he set them in their courses in relation to the birth of one man …Such a man we must see …And when we see him, we shall all worship before his face."

"Master Melchior! …What is that glow in the cloud over the palace?"

"It is the Morning Star my son."

"It's very bright!"

"Yes, it is the brightest of all the stars because it declares the rising of the sun."

As the cloud moves away, Babylon is lit up by the brightest star ever seen. Breathtaking in beauty, it climbs up into the eastern sky. So brilliant is its light, that it can still be seen during the day…

"Ahi, there has never been a star such as this one. The sun is well up and it is still visible," says Caspar, wiping the sweat off his brow.

"I never thought I'd see the day we'd be watching a star at high noon."

Balthazar, looking intently into the sky, shielding his eyes from the sun, at length, answers…

"It is two stars. I see two stars. Jupiter is with it, and it is leading to the west. We have a direction."

"If that other star is Jupiter, then it will be the same again tomorrow. If it is the same, that will be enough for me," says Caspar, his implication plain to all.

"Yes ahi, we shall inform the ashshawph immediately. Shall we take the apprentices with us?" asks Melchior with a twinkle in his eye.

"Master; how could you say such a thing …of course you will take us with you! Does all our training have no purpose? If you leave us behind I will never forgive you!"

The three burst into laughter at the seriousness of Ghina's reaction.

Once the Council of the Magi had settled the matter, it still took three months to prepare for the expedition. Camels and supplies for 45 men plus servants and guards was quite an undertaking even in Babylon. It was a small army that eventually rode out into the western desert following that star…

✽ ✽ ✽ ✽ ✽

Now after Jesus was born in Bethlehem of Judea in the days of Herod the king, magi from the east arrived in Jerusalem, saying, "Where is He who has been born King of the Jews? For we saw His star in the east and have come to worship Him."

When Herod the king heard this, he was troubled, and all Jerusalem with him.

Gathering together all the chief priests and scribes of the people, he inquired of them where the Messiah was to be born. They said to him, "In Bethlehem of Judea; for this is what has been written by the prophet: 'and you, Bethlehem, land of Judah, are by no means least among the leaders of Judah; for out of you shall come forth a ruler who will shepherd my people Israel.'"

Then Herod secretly called the magi and determined from them the exact time the star appeared. And he sent them to Bethlehem and said, "Go and search carefully for the Child; and when you have found Him, report to me, so that I too may come and worship Him."

After hearing the king, they went their way; and the star, which they had seen in the east, went on before them until it came and stood over the place where the Child was.

When they saw the star, they rejoiced exceedingly with great joy. After coming into the house they saw the Child with Mary His mother; and they fell to the ground and worshiped Him. Then, opening their treasures, they presented to Him gifts of gold, frankincense, and myrrh. And having been warned by God in a dream not to return to Herod, the magi left for their own country by another way.

Now when they had gone, behold, an angel of the Lord appeared to Joseph in a dream and said, "Get up! Take the Child and His mother and flee to Egypt, and remain there until I tell you; for Herod is going to search for the Child to destroy Him."

So Joseph got up and took the Child and His mother while it was still night, and left for Egypt. He remained there until the death of Herod. This was to fulfill what had been spoken by the Lord through the prophet: "Out of Egypt I called my Son."

Then when Herod saw that he had been tricked by the magi, he became very enraged, and sent and slew all the male children who were in Bethlehem and all its vicinity, from two years old and under, according to the time which he had determined from the magi.

Then what had been spoken through Jeremiah the prophet was fulfilled: "A voice was heard in Ra-

mah, weeping and great morning, Rachel weeping for her children; and she refused to be comforted; because they were no more."

But when Herod died, behold, an angel of the Lord appeared in a dream to Joseph in Egypt, and said, "Get up, take the Child and His mother, and go into the land of Israel; for those who sought the Child's life are dead."

So Joseph got up, took the Child and His mother, and came into the land of Israel. But when he heard that Archelaus was reigning over Judea in place of his father Herod, he was afraid to go there. Then after being warned by God in a dream, he left for the regions of Galilee, and came and lived in a city called Nazareth.

This was to fulfill what was spoken through the prophets: "He shall be called a Nazarene." (Matthew 2 NASU)

� ✻ ✻ ✻ ✻ ✻

www.kingdomgatespublishing.com

Other Books by Colin Baker

from The Voice Series:

The Voice in Galatians

The Voice in 1 Thessalonians

The Voice in 2 Thessalonians

The Voice in 1 Corinthians

...with more to come.

from The Gates of the Kingdom Series:

The Gates of the Kingdom Part 1

The Gates of the Kingdom Part 2

The Gates of the Kingdom Part 3

...with more to come.

These titles and more are available in PDF, ePub and Audio format for Laptop, Tablet and Mobile devices from www.colininthespirit.com.

About the Author

Colin Baker lives in Australia's Northern Territory in the remote Aboriginal Homeland Community of Gäwa.

Gäwa is a name well loved. It's origins are Macassan. It means 'Land of the King'.

His experience at Gäwa has been one of pioneering and gate-keeping, perseverance, patience and overcoming.

He is committed to the glory of God as is reflected in his vision to facilitate an embracing of the Gospel of the Glory by God's people.

His mandate is pictured in Ezekiel chapter one when viewed in the light of the fact that 'movement in the Spiritual Realm is by vision'. ...And that the Lord's Community is the vehicle that transports the throne and the One seated upon it into all the Earth.

from The Gates of the Kingdom Book Series

www.ingramcontent.com/pod-product-compliance
Lightning Source LLC
Chambersburg PA
CBHW071411040426
42444CB00009B/2195